Awakening the Dragon

THE DRAGON BOAT FESTIVAL

ARLENE CHAN

ILLUSTRATED BY

SONG NAN ZHANG

Tundra Books

Published in Canada by Tundra Books,
75 Sherbourne Street, Toronto, Ontario M5A 2P9

Published in the United States by Tundra Books of Northern New York,
P.O. Box 1030, Plattsburgh, New York 12901

Library of Congress Control Number: 2003113654

Library and Archives of Canada Cataloguing in Publication

Chan, Arlene
    Awakening the dragon / Arlene Chan ; illustrated by Son Nan Zhang.

ISBN-13 978-0-88776-805-7 (pbk.)
ISBN-13 978-0-88776-656-5 (bound)
ISBN-10 0-88776-656-0 (bound)

    1. Dragon boat festival — Juvenile literature. I. Zhang, Song Nan, 1942-
II. Title.

GT4883.A2C43 2004   j394.2'6951   C2003-905877-8

We acknowledge the financial support of the Government of Canada through
the Book Publishing Industry Development Program (BPIDP) and that of
the Government of Ontario through the Ontario Media Development
Corporation's Ontario Book Initiative. We further acknowledge the support
of the Canada Council for the Arts and the Ontario Arts Council for our
publishing program.

ONTARIO ARTS COUNCIL
CONSEIL DES ARTS DE L'ONTARIO

Printed and bound in Hong Kong, China

1 2 3 4 5 6   12 11 10 09 08 07

TO MY FAMILY, ESPECIALLY MY MOM

Special thanks to kennyp

A. C.

TO THE MEMORY OF MY PARENTS

S. N. Z.

Honoring the River Dragon

Dragons have been a symbol of Chinese culture for
thousands of years. The ancient Chinese believed that
each river and lake had guardian dragons living in palaces
deep in the waters. Dragons were usually well-meaning
creatures, protectors of the people. But when they were
angry, dragons wreaked havoc. They brought too much rain, with
floods and storms, or no rain at all. For this reason, it was important
to keep the River Dragon happy. Sacrifices were made to the River
Dragon so that it would, in return, bring the right amount of rain.

Since ancient times, Chinese festivals have been celebrated in pur-
suit of happiness and good health. They were set long ago according to
the sowing and reaping of crops. The Dragon Boat Festival occurs

when young rice shoots have been planted and the summer rains are about to begin.

To honor the River Dragon, long, narrow boats were built in its image. The dragon head held a prominent position at the bow. It was a ferocious-looking creature with the head of a camel, the horns of a stag, the eyes of a demon, the neck of a snake, and the ears of a cow.

Fierce races were held in the belief that they would bring prosperous and bountiful crops. The competitions became a tradition of the rain-making festival, which took place at the beginning of the summer. Dragon boat races were not connected with the Dragon Boat Festival until the Han dynasty (206 BC – 220 AD).

Some people say the Dragon Boat Festival started with the ancient worship of the River Dragon and the dragon boat races. Others believe it began in memory of one of China's famous poets, Qu Yuan.

The Poet Qu Yuan

*L*ong ago in a time known as the Warring States period, there were seven kingdoms in China, each fighting against the other for supremacy. The largest and most powerful kingdoms were Chu and Qin.

Chu was ruled by a king who surrounded himself with many advisors. Qu Yuan was one of the king's most trusted and respected counselors. He was highly regarded by the people.

In those turbulent times, court intrigues ran rampant. Corrupt advisors were jealous of Qu Yuan's favored position with the king. Because he was a man of high moral standing, they could not find a way to discredit him.

Qu Yuan's position would not last forever. The enemy kingdom of Qin had prepared a peace agreement that Qu Yuan suspected was a trap. Having the best interests of his people at heart, he advised the king against signing it. His recommendation was to be his downfall.

Jealous advisors, eager to rid the court of this popular statesman, accused Qu Yuan of disloyalty and treason. The king of Chu did not listen to Qu Yuan's wise advice and signed the peace agreement. Moreover, he banished Qu Yuan from the kingdom.

For twenty lonely years, Qu Yuan wandered aimlessly about the countryside. Bearing the burden of his dishonorable exile, he expressed his continued love for his king and people through his poetry.

Qu Yuan lost all hope when he heard the worst news. His beloved kingdom, Chu, was conquered by the brutal Qin army. Qu Yuan, in utter despair, clutched a huge rock to his chest and threw himself into the Mi Luo River. It was the fifth day of the fifth month.

Word of Qu Yuan's drowning spread quickly. Hundreds of villagers raced out in their boats to try to search for the body of their beloved statesman, but they were too late. They splashed the waters with their paddles and banged loudly on their drums to keep the River Dragon from devouring him. They scattered rice into the river so that Qu Yuan's spirit would not go hungry.

Bringing Good Fortune

*T*he Dragon Boat Festival falls on the fifth day of the fifth month in the lunar calendar. It is also called the Festival of the Double Fifth and is considered the unluckiest day of the year. The fifth month, occuring in May or June in the western calendar, is considered an evil month that brings misfortune and disease. Five Gods of Plague roam the earth during this month. In ancient times, these were the evil spirits that brought bad luck.

To protect against misfortune, many customs developed and continue today. During the Dragon Boat Festival, families hang garlic or branches of fragrant herbs, such as mugwort or calamus, above their doorways. The mugwort leaf looks like a tiger, the supreme protector against evil spirits. The calamus leaf looks like a demon-killing sword.

Realgar, an ancient folk medicine, is burned. Its yellow smoke and noxious smell drive away evil spirits. Realgar is also added to food to ward off disease.

Fragrant pouches, or *xiangbao*, protect their wearers from illness. Made of colorful cotton or silk and filled with dried flowers and herbs, these are very popular with children, who collect as many as possible. Children also wear bracelets of five-colored threads or five-colored ribbons in their hair. These are called "threads of long life" or "threads for prolonging life." The five colors each represent the five elements or natural forces: blue for wood, red for fire, yellow for earth, white for metal, and black for water.

The five "poisons" also fight bad luck. These creatures are the centipede, lizard, scorpion, snake, and toad. The five poisons are used to decorate clothing, quilts, bags, and even cakes, for protection against their fatal bites.

Feeding the Dragon

*T*he most popular custom during the Dragon Boat Festival is the making and eating of rice dumplings, or *zongzi*. Legend has it that *zongzi* were first used by the fishermen to feed the spirit of Qu Yuan. Others say that the *zongzi* were offered to the River Dragon during the festival. A content River Dragon brought the right amount of rainfall for the farmers.

*Zong*zi are made with soft, sticky rice that is wrapped in bamboo leaves and tied with string. They vary by region both in shape and filling. In Beijing, they are shaped like triangles and filled with sweet fillings such as bean paste, walnuts, and dates. In southern China, the smallest of the *zongzi* resemble little pillows and are made with a strong alkaline solution known as *jian shui*. The third variety, also from the South, has four sides with round or pointed corners. It is made with a savory filling such as chicken, peanuts, or salted duck egg and is available year-round in Chinese stores, bakeries, and restaurants. When you cut away the string and unwrap the bamboo leaves, you are treated to a heavenly feast fit for the River Dragon.

The Demon Slayer

Of all the customs observed during the Dragon Boat Festival, none is more frightening than the appearance of Zhong Kui, the demon slayer.

According to legend, Emperor Minghuang (712-756) tossed and turned in his imperial bed one night. He was burning with fever but the court physicians could do nothing to quell the fires in his body. He was tormented in a nightmare by a demon who was dressed in red, with one shoe on and one shoe off. Suddenly, a tall ghost appeared. Dressed in the robes, hat, and black boots of a scholar, he gouged out one of the demon's eyes and ate it with great relish. He then crushed the creature with his bare hands.

The mysterious figure identified himself as Zhong Kui. In life, he had been unjustly prevented from becoming an advisor in Emperor Minghuang's court. Out of shame, he committed suicide, thus becoming a wandering ghost, or *kui*. Because the emperor gave him a funeral fit for royalty, Zhong Kui swore to forever be the emperor's guardian spirit and to free the world of evil ghosts and demons.

The emperor awoke from his dream, his fever gone. He ordered the court artist to paint the image of Zhong Kui, his protector. What was captured most dramatically was the demon slayer's fierce, bulging eyes. This image predominates the walls of households to ward off evil spirits during the Festival of the Double Fifth.

Awakening the Dragon

Dragon boats commemorate the tragic end of Qu Yuan. They represent the boats of the villagers who raced in a desperate attempt to save him from drowning. Ranging from thirty to one hundred feet in length, dragon boats are wide enough to fit two people side by side. Traditional dragon boats are made out of teakwood, while modern ones are made of fiberglass. A fierce-looking dragon head is at the prow, a tail at the stern. Scales are painted in the traditional colors of red, yellow, and green, red being the most predominant.

The traditional awakening of the dragon is a colorful ceremony of the dragon boat races. This ancient ritual is held for newly built dragon boats and also for boats that have been "sleeping" in storage between races.

Taoist priests begin the ceremony by chanting to scare away evil spirits and to bring good luck to the race course, the competitors, and their dragon boats. Paper money, incense, and candles are burned, and food and wine are displayed on an altar.

To awaken the dragon boats from their deep sleep, Taoist priests or invited guests from the community dot the eyes of the dragon with red paint.

The Dragon Boat Team

The rules for dragon boat races vary depending on the size of the dragon boats and the length of the race course. Typically, a dragon boat team is made up of twenty paddlers, a drummer, and a steersperson. The paddlers, sitting in pairs, provide the power that drives the dragon boat through the water. The first three rows of paddlers are called the "pacers." The middle rows are called the "engine." The paddlers at the back of the boat are called the "rockets" or "terminators."

Dragon boat teams are made up of men, women, students, and mixed teams of all ages and abilities. There was a time, however, when only men were allowed to compete. The Chinese believed that all things in the universe were male (*yang*) or female (*yin*). The powerful dragon represented all things male. Allowing women to participate in dragon boat races would have angered the River God. Women raced separately in phoenix boats. The phoenix, a mythological bird of great beauty, was the symbol of the female.

Preparing for the Races

*D*ragon boat racing is a strenuous activity that requires endurance, technique, timing and teamwork. To build endurance, paddlers prepare with strength training and aerobic exercises such as jogging and cycling. Endurance is important to give the strength and stamina to finish the race.

Even paddlers with good endurance will tire quickly without the proper technique. The paddling stroke can be broken down into several parts, each designed to achieve maximum power and speed. Hours are spent practicing the technique of a perfect stroke.

Timing, or paddling in unison with the boat crew, is also critical for success. If the timing is off, a paddle may clash with another in front or behind. When the timing is perfect, the dragon boat surges at each stroke and flies through the water.

Teamwork, the last key element of training, pulls everything together. Paddlers must follow the pacers in the front three rows, listen to the drummer, and focus on their strokes . . . all the time working in perfect harmony as a team.

The Dragon Boat Race

*T*he dragon boats are lined up in their race lanes. There is a hush among the spectators. The teams await the signal for the race to begin. It will be a cannon blast, a gunshot, or the honk of a starter's horn. *Paddles up!* The paddlers are poised to attack the water. *Race ready!* The teams position the tips of their paddles in the water in readiness for the first powerful pull. If there is any movement of the paddlers after this point, the team is disqualified. The tension mounts. *BANG!* The race is on.

A surge of energy drives the dragon boats forward from a dead stop. The first few strokes are deep and strong to pull the dragon boat out of the water as much as possible. These strokes are followed by the sprint, a series of fast race strokes that get the boat up to racing speed. There is a frenzied sea of arms and paddles, each team paddling in harmony. Within seconds, the dragon boats are like arrows flying through the water. The team settles in for a steady race pace of long, strong strokes.

The steersperson maneuvers the straightest course from the start to the finish lines. If the dragon boat strays into another race lane, the team is disqualified. The paddlers focus their energy as one team, the sound of their drum pulsing like the heart of the mighty dragon.

The finish line approaches. The drummer decides at precisely what point the team must make its final effort. The paddlers are nearing complete exhaustion, their arms and bodies crying out for the end of the race. At the drummer's command, the team increases the stroke rate. The paddlers use every last ounce of energy. The dragon boat crosses the finish line. The race is over.

The winning teams raise their paddles triumphantly above their heads. In the spirit of fun and sportsmanship, the racers splash each other. According to an old custom, likely from the Water Splashing Festival, paddlers believe that the wetter they become, the happier they will be.

Spectators cheer for the teams. Their enthusiasm for one of the fastest growing sports is echoed around the world in countries like New Zealand, the Philippines, England, Germany, the United States, and Canada. Thousands of paddlers and spectators come together every year to participate in the rich cultural traditions of the Dragon Boat Festival.

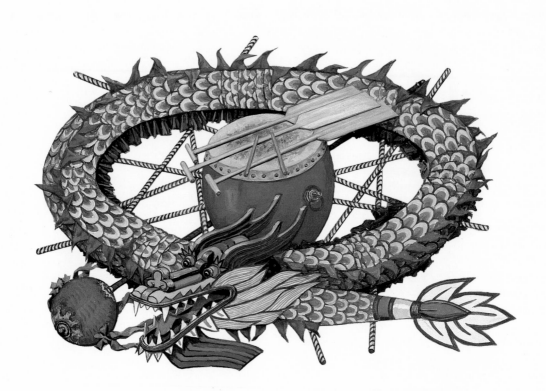